Thomas Erskine

Observations on the prevailing abuses in the British army,

Arising from the corruption of civil government, with a proposal to the

officers towards obtaining an addition to their pay

Thomas Erskine

Observations on the prevailing abuses in the British army,
Arising from the corruption of civil government, with a proposal to the officers towards obtaining an addition to their pay

ISBN/EAN: 9783337713775

Printed in Europe, USA, Canada, Australia, Japan

Cover: Foto ©ninafisch / pixelio.de

More available books at **www.hansebooks.com**

OBSERVATIONS

ON THE

PREVAILING ABUSES

IN THE

BRITISH ARMY,

ARISING FROM THE

CORRUPTION of CIVIL GOVERNMENT.

WITH A

PROPOSAL to the OFFICERS

towards obtaining an Addition to their Pay.

By the Honourable * * * ——— an Officer.

Si omnes voluimus, quod arguimur, non diftinguimus volun-
tatem a facto : Omnes plectamur.   TIT. LIV. lib. xlv.

———

LONDON,

Printed for T. DAVIES, in Ruffel-ftreet, Covent-garden;
and J. BEW, in Pater-nofter-Row.
MDCCLXXV.

OBSERVATIONS, &c.

THERE is no tafk more difficult than to combat, with fuccefs, abufes of long ftanding ; they borrow the appearance of right from immemorial cuftom, and it is almoft impoffible to roufe men to acute feelings of fufferings and oppreffions, of which they themfelves have not feen, or felt the beginnings.

But evils are ftill more infurmountable, when their removal demands a fteady and prompt unanimity, in extenfive communities. The various interefts and opinions of men defeat the completion of this moft powerful engine of human force ; and

B   great

great reformations are confequently either the fruits of long, and often fruftrated labours, or the birth of fortunate accidents.

There may be, perhaps, two caufes of the many feeble, ill-concerted, and worfe fupported attempts, towards an augmentation of the pay of the Britifh troops, which feem now to be fo fubmiffively, or indolently laid afide, and the grievance, with many others, fo patiently fupported, that to offer new propofals on the fubject, cannot but carry with it the air of quixotifm.

But as attempts that have been deemed unwarrantable from improbability of fuccefs, have often been found to be very eafy on trial, and their apparent difficulties to be only the bugbears of irrefolution, ardent enterprifing fpirits are fometimes eminently ufeful as pioneers to regular and fober

ber induſtry ; men who have virtue
and talents for executing work which
is put into their hands, have not always fertile and progreſſive inventions,
but treat every thing as impoſſible and
chimerical, which preſents any glaring difficulties ; and the world would
ſtand ſtill, and every ſpecies of improvement be at an end, if nature did not
provide another ſet of men, of irritable
and reſtleſs diſpoſitions, fretful under
grievances, and ambitious of being the
inſtruments of public advantage.

It is this diſpoſition and perhaps
this ambition, which lead me to addreſs myſelf to the officers of the Britiſh army; to demonſtrate to them how
ſhamefully, from the preſent miſerable
eſtabliſhment of their pay, and other
glaring abuſes, they are cut off from
their ſhare in the proſperities of Great
Britain ; to ſhew to them, how far this
inſulting misfortune is owing to their

abſurd

abfurd neglect of their own advantages, and to endeavour to roufe
them to a fpirited, yet conftitutional demand of the juft rights of her moft ufeful and laborious citizens.

At firft view, this may appear to
be a dangerous fubject, and highly
incompatible with the arbitrary principles of military government. What
is termed Remonftrance in a citizen,
is fuppofed to be Mutiny in a foldier;
but mutiny, I apprehend to be con-
fined to the breach of difcipline and
fubordination in an inferior, towards
a fuperior in military command.
Soldiers do not give up their general
rights as members of a free community; they are amenable to civil
and municipal laws, as well as to their
own martial code, and are therefore
entitled to all the privileges with which
a free form of government invefts every
individual: nay, it is to their virtue,
that

that all the other parts of the community muſt ultimately truſt for the enjoyment of their peaceable privileges. For as Mr. Pitt (now Lord Chatham), in his ſtrong figurative eloquence expreſſed himſelf in parliament, " To the " virtue of the army we have hither- " to truſted ; to that virtue, ſmall as " the army is, we muſt ſtill truſt ; and " without that virtue, the lords, the " commons, and the people of Eng- " land may intrench themſelves be- " hind parchment up to the teeth, but " the ſword will find a paſſage to the " vitals of the conſtitution."

There is nothing really dangerous in this ſeemingly alarming truth. The people of England have been often impoſed upon by dark and deſigning men, to regard the army with a jealous and malignant eye, as the ſurly tool of arbitrary power, and the foe of liberty. The faults of indi-

viduals

viduals have been unthinkingly charged on the whole body, and the execution of civil juſtice too often re-
quiring the ſupport of military force
(the moſt hateful and reluctant duty
of an Engliſh ſoldier), has ſown the
ſeeds of diſcord and ſuſpicion between two branches of the community, equally neceſſary and reſpectable ;
between the law and its protectors,
between the people and their brethren
and defenders. But notwithſtanding
this jealouſy ſo much to be lamented, there is nothing reaſonably to be
feared from a ſtanding army of double the number of the preſent. The
army is, I believe, as zealous for the
real proſperity and freedom of Great
Britain, as any other collective body
in the nation ; it is by her own corrupt
repreſentatives, that the axe has been
laid to the root of her liberties—It is
in the ſenate, and not the barracks,
of

of the kingdom, that the pillars of the conſtitution have been ſhaken—It is from thence that the people have ſuffered—it is from thence that the army has been oppreſſed.

The great and principal reaſon why the deaf ear has ſtill been preſented to the petitions of the army, is, becauſe no diſagreeable conſequences have reſulted from the neglect of them. Parliament ſees, equally with ourſelves, the juſtice and urgency of our expectations ; the legiſlators of Great Britain know very well, that the officers in the army cannot ſupport that appearance which is expected from gentlemen, and that the whole eſtabliſhment of the pay is mean and ſcandalous; but we have never proved to them that it is requiſite in policy to redreſs theſe grievances ; we have truſted alone to the force of truth and juſtice,which ſeldom have pleaded ſuc-

ceſsfully

cefsfully in any public affembly of men, unlefs neceffity and intereft fupported them; and fo far are thefe from being our advocates in the prefent cafe, that our own folly turns them as arguments and weapons againft us.

I need not inform the gentlemen of the army, nor indeed the public in general, that, except in regiments ftationed in remote and noxious climates, a vacancy of even an enfigncy for purchafe, is feldom without more than one candidate, although the pay is little more, in proportion to the purchafe money, than what the fame fum, funk in a fafe fund, would annually procure, without the obligation of fervice, or the flavery of fubordination. The progreffive fteps muft now almoft in every inftance be feverely purchafed on the fame difadvantageous terms as the firft, and even then are feldom procured but

with

with greater difficulty, and more
ftretch of what is ftyled parliamentary
intereft, than would raife a gentleman
to opulence and independence in any
other purfuit, or profeffion; and when
the top of the ladder is gained, the
emoluments bear no proportion to the
expences infeparable from military
parade, or even to the common neceffaries and comforts of life. No
refpect is gained, no honour reflect-
ed, and no weight, or confideration
is acquired in the country ; neverthelefs the ftandards are flocked to with
tumultuous emulation.

When infatuation thus prevails
over common fenfe, and the vanity
of youth is fowing thorns for the pil-
low of age; when the glitter of a
brafs gorget effaces even the folid
luftre of gold ; and the fafh, that too
juft emblem of an empty purfe, is
preferred to the fcarf, or toga, is it

C   wonder-

wonderful that parliament ſhould not redreſs the grievances of the army? is it wonderful that men, who have forced themſelves by corruption into the chair of authority, ſhould not throw the ſpoils from them, on the heads of men who are not even looking for them?

Places and penſions multiply yearly in ſuch an aſtoniſhing ratio, that, without a ſudden ſtop, nay a radical cure of theſe running ſores of corruption, not only the pay of the army muſt remain unaugmented, but in time the army muſt be diſbanded. G——t is at preſent in the ſituation of a hard drinker : when wine, from inordinate uſe, becomes too cold for the ſtomach, he flies to rum, from rum to brandy, and thus runs the climax through all the ſtages of fermentation. The powerful cordials of ſtate which were not formerly adminiſtered

except

except on urgent occasions, are now
become the habitual regimen of every
fenator. A member of the H--- of
C——— can no more live without a
place, or penfion, than a peerefs without her maccaroni, or a chambermaid
her perquifites. The traders ob-
ferve this, and raife the prices of their
commodities ; the money-dealers
lower the interest of their funds ; the
manufacturers double the wages of
their labour ; the hufbandman refufes
to plough the land, and the mariner
the fea, till the farmer and the mer-
chant keep up the proportion between
the value of money and the neceffities
of life. The foldier alone, with hol-
low eye and haggard cheek, fmiles
contented on his fcarlet, hated by the
populace as the fuppofed tool of
defpotifm, yet neglected by government as the voluntary and unworthy
flave.

C 2   The

The crown indeed very wifely a-
vails itfelf of the fpirit, or rather folly
of the times ; and as a nurfe with a
bad breaft of milk hufhes a ftarving
infant with a rattle, it rings all the
changes on buckram and buttons,
and buttons and buckram, to pleafe
the warriors of Blackheath and Wim-
bledon, and to fpread wider the con-
tagion of the *fcarlet fever*, which is
nearly fynonimous with the *goal
diftemper*.

To enter into a detail of the
taxes, which the progrefs of luxury and the advancement of commerce have laid on the decencies
and neceffities of life fince the eftablifhment of the army was formed, would not only be tedioufly need-
lefs, to fuch as are acquainted with
the hiftory of Great Britain, but to
perfons of all denominations ; who
from their own memories can draw
fuf-

fufficient comparifons, to make a ftriking eftimate of the fituation of military officers, more efpecially in the fubaltern ranks of the profeffion. It may however be proper to remark, that fince the above mentioned period, two new worlds, the fources of almoft all the delicacies of nature, and the enchantments of luxury, have, like two immenfe torrents, overwhelmed the commercial nations of Europe, fwept away the very traces of œconomy and fimplicity of manners, and fo metamorphofed the face and appearance of things, that could our forefathers arife from the manfions of the dead, they would be at a lofs to recognize either their country or their children. The fober fons of induftry, apparelled and fed by the manufactures and productions of England, fupported by ftaffs, the growth of her native woods, now glitter in the borrowed

rowed plumes of Afia and America, grow wanton with her fpices and con- fections, and roll along the broadened ways in gilded chariots. The emi- grants return in multitudes from the other hemifphere, laden with the fpoils of murder, barbarity, and de- folation, mount into the feats of ho- nour, and ftamp the fterling mark on vice and extravagance.

Whatever is for a while upheld by the authority of univerfal cuftom, foon interweaves itfelf with nature, and is confidered as one of her in- nate demands. The expenfive com- modities of the two Indies, and the hourly births of inventive pride and prodigal fenfuality, fland in this de- lufive predicament. The want of them cannot be atoned for by the moft exemplary virtue, or the moft public utility. There is no refource in the funds of human wifdom and

6

refo-

refolution to withftand the tyranny
of fafhion. All the actions and opinions of mankind are whirled round
in this irrefiftible vortex; the moft
noble and virtuous minds are the moft
ftrongly fufceptible of even a falfe
fenfe of fhame; fenfibility, the conftant companion of worth, is too trem-
blingly awake to be compofedly happy under the unmerited contempt of
even defpicable objects. Hence the
pangs of poverty have been felt moft a-
cutely, where the gnawings of hunger
and the cold of nakednefs have fcarce
made any impreffion; thefe corporeal
fufferings bear no proportion to the
keen fenfations of honeft minds, when
their birth and fituation are not the o-
pen paffports of their diftrefs. The la-
bourer, whom difeafe or idlenefs has
reduced to indigence, demands the
poor-rates in his parifh, or, trufting
to the eloquence of mifery, throws
himfelf

himself into the haunts of men, and
subsists on the tribute of compassion;
he feels no shame in the importuni-
ties of beggary, the cravings of nature
are his only sufferings, and from these
he is soon relieved; for to the eter-
nal honour of Great Britain, the rich
are in a manner the stewards of providence for the protection of the poor.

But the horrors of indigence in
the higher walks of life are of a
different kind, and are much more
deplorable. They are such as should
never be felt, but as the scourges of
indolence, or the retribution of dif-
honesty: it is a disgrace to the government, and to the nation, where poverty is the squalid associate of the
most laborious of the public servants
who live within the pale of death
for the defence of their country; give
up all the happy rights of free men,
and, for the common cause, subject
them-

themselves voluntarily to a government, compared with which, even Turkey is a republic.

Officers in the army, even in the most subaltern ranks, have the misfortune to be considered as gentlemen; which in England, as in other countries, implies a denomination of persons, who from the accidental circumstance of office, or property, are divided from the common herd of mankind, and are obliged to form a barrier between these two orders, (as there is none in nature,) by the luxuries of dress, equipage, and attendance; but as the superfluities of life are the only props to this order of society, it is evident how distressing it must be to be installed in it, unfurnished with the very articles to which it owes its existence. The vulgar must be paid for the superiority assumed by their betters; the advan-

D   tages

tages which they receive from the cir-
culation of fuperabundancies, is the
only charter men have for refpect in
a free country; and whenever that is
wanting, the jealoufy, and independent fpirit of the multitude drags
them to a level. When the journey-
man taylor, weaver, or any common
mechanic, can live on his wages
more refpectably than the officer in
the army; the fcarlet and embroidery lofe their luftre, and become the
derifion of the dregs of the people.

An Englifh officer, in the opinion
of the multitude, bears the fame proportion to a gentleman, as a poor
knight of Windfor does to a companion
of the order of the garter.

The fituation of an officer whofe
fervices have not been rewarded by
promotion, is truly deplorable. Often
thrown behind in his circumftances
by unavoidable expences, incompatible
with

with his finances, and his income at
the same time so small, that the most
rigid self-denial cannot allot a part
for accumulation : his misery is ir-
revocable, and the most flight misfortune, or imprudence is ruin : he
must either shut himself up from
happinefs and society, or involve himself deeper; he must either fret away
his life in the hectic of fenfibility,
or pine in the gloom of despair.
If, by uncommon circumfpection, he
avoids this Scylla and Charybdis of
poverty, he may exist, but cannot be
said to live : no recreation in the
walk of a gentleman is within his
compafs ; in the mean time, years
and infirmities creep on apace, with
the chagrining retrofpect of a youth
fpent without pleafure, and without
profit, and the dismal profpect of an
old age of want and obfcurity.

D 2

I ap-

I appeal to all officers who have no private property, and who confequently have not been promoted, whether or not I have drawn a faithful portrait of the profeffion ?

The private foldier in his line, has the fame comparative fufferings, and mortifications with the officer; if the painful feelings which are only the taxes on refined manners, are not his portion, they are made up in the real wants and fufferings of animal nature. From the eight pence per day, which is iffued for the pay of the foldier, when the deductions are made, for cloathing, for neceffaries, for wafhing, for the pay-mafter, for the furgeon, and the multiplied articles of ufelefs and unmilitary fopperies, (introduced by many colonels, to the oppreffion of the foldier, for what they call the credit and appearance of the regiment;) there is not a

fuffisufficient overplus for healthful subsistence, under the most salutary regulations: and as to the little enjoyments and recreations, which even the meanest rank of men can call their own in any country, the brave, the honourable, the veteran soldier, must not aspire to. Yet in those men, we expect romantic spirit, heroic fortitude, point of honour, and the love of their country ; principles which can but feebly exist, when the body is reduced from monastic abstinence, and the ardour of the mind is broken with neglect and oppression. The characters, and capabilities of men, are not only influenced, but absolutely changed from circumstance and situation ; they neither depend totally on the mind, or on the body, but on their mutual operation on each other, as they are differently actuated. There is nearly as much mechanism in our

ra-

rational exertions, as in the inftinct of
animals; and foldiers may be as much
formed by art to undaunted enter-
prife, or funk into cowards from the
want of it, as horfes may be trained
to rufh upon fixed bayonets, or be
fcared _fo as to ftart at their fha-
dows.

Butcher's meat and bread, are at
prefent four times the prices they
were when the pay was firft eftablifh-
ed; and every abfolute necefliry of
life in the fame proportion, from the
decreafe of the value of money, the
extenfive commerce, and riches of the
kingdom, and the great taxes which
have fince been laid on every article
of univerfal confumption. A fhilling
and eighteen pence per day is now the
common rate of labour: mechanics and
journeymen, tradefmen of all denominations, exact at leaft two fhillings
and half a crown from their employ-

I   ers;

ers; and so inadequate are even these additional prices to the expences of living, that population decreases, and the kingdom is emaciated by continual and alarming emigrations. As luxury stalks on with more progressive strides, the wants of mankind are multiplied; they, in consequence, refuse their labour, till these new wants are supplied; well knowing that the different necessaries, and luxuries of life, to which their labour is directed, cannot stand still, but must wait on their nod: this change is not prejudicial to their employers, who charge it, with interest, on manufactures and commodities, which they sell reciprocally to each other, and to land-holders; which last, to supply the deficiencies and the calls of new luxuries, raise their farms, and put them into the hands of oppulent monopolizers: these, uniformly attached

to

to their own interests, make up, in
their turns, for the extraordinary rents,
and the increased expence of cultivation, and utensils, by raising the corn
to exorbitant prices, which, when the
poor are unable to purchase, they
transport to foreign countries, not-
withstanding the constant laws which
pass to prevent them.

In this active and mutable scene,
in this fermentation of commerce,
amidst the innumerable inventions and
chicanery of men, to evade poverty,
and to acquire riches, whilst the natural progress of society is fabricating
continual changes, and these changes
have obliged men of all denominations to fall into new channels of operation; in this long chain of human
necessities which have increased and
fattened on each other, still rising, but
rising in equable proportions, (as a
tune is still the same, though played
on a higher key;) what must be the lot
of

of one link which fticks faft in fo rapid a wheel? Like a fhip which is aground in a tempeft, it muft be fpeedily deftroyed. To fay that this is unfortunately the cafe of the Britifh army, is not to have difcovered a wonderful enigma; it is indeed the ftranded and difmafted hulk, who, while the fleet around, with the ufe of fails and rudders, fight fafely againft the tumultuous conflict, is dafhed againft the rocks into ten thoufand pieces.

But thefe circumftances are not alone fhamefully unjuft, and oppreffive of a moft valuable part of the community; they may be traced further in their confequences, and may eafily be proved to be as highly impolitical, as hurtful to the ftate, befide being totally deftructive of the army.

Whenever, from a want of due diftribution of national advantage, any portion of the community does not receive

E   its

its equitable dividend, all zeal for the
public good muſt neceſſarily languiſh
in that quarter; for perſonal advantages, and valuable privileges, are the
ſources of the moſt refined and rational patriotiſm. The more important then and extenſive this portion is,
which is thus cut off from the main
body by unjuſt and fraudulent depri-
vation, the more the ſtate ſuffers in its
intereſts: if the commercial branch is
clogged with oppreſſive monopolies,
prohibitions, and taxations, trade de-
cays, and the conſequence is poverty.
If the military body is held in diſre-
pute, its eſtabliſhments meaſured
out by the narrow hand of ungene-
rous œconomy, and the wreath of honour made ſubſervient to corruption,
the power of a ſtate is weakened from
the apoſtacy of its defenders; and thus
a kingdom may languiſh into poverty,
or be overwhelmed in conqueſt. The
latter

latter confequence is immediately in point, and deferves a ferious difcuffion.

From the miferable eftablifhment of pay, the expences of military parade, and the impoffibility of rifing without parliamentary intereft, the number of officers, who embrace the army ferioufly as a profeffion, daily decreafes, and thofe who ftill do, remain for the moft part in the fubaltern ranks, and are never heard of: thofe who fucceed in it, are in general cadets of opulent families, and fometimes perfons of great wealth, and landed property ; but I appeal to the army, and to the nation, if thefe men often deferve the honourable title of foldiers? A commiffion, and a tour through Italy, are the finifhing ftrokes to modern education ; they are undertaken with the fame ferious intention, and are profecuted with equal improvement.

So

So long as the battalions are en-
camped on native plains, or immured
in peaceful ʼbarracks, ſo long thoſe
ſons of riot and effeminacy maintain
their poſts. The brilliant orbit of
Ranelagh glows with their ſcarlet,
and the avenues of Vauxhall glitter
with blades drawn againſt unarmed
apprentices in honour of a ſtrumpet,
which ruſt in their ſcabbards when
their country calls : if for a review, or
a muſter, they are obliged to loll in
their vis à-vis to the quarters of their
regiment, it is but to enflame the
contempt and hatred of the people of England againſt the defenders
of their peaceable privileges. They
gallop again to town, after having
filled the country with ſuch horror at
their diſhonourable debaucheries, that
hoſpitable doors are ſhut againſt
officers of principle and reputation.

Such are the advantages which the
military profeſſion reaps from theſe
apes in embroidery ; ſuch are the he-
roes, that in the event of a war, muſt
lead the Britiſh troops to battle : for
theſe men riſe almoſt univerſally over
the heads of officers grey with fatigues, and rough with ſcars, whoſe
courage and abilities yet preſerve the honour of the Engliſh name ; who, without money, and without intereſt, languiſh in the ſubaltern ranks, unknown
and unreſpected, who hardly live under the throbbings of hearts, wound-
ed from ſenſibility, and broken with
diſappointment ; and after having
braved all the terrors and calamities
of war, and immortalized their country, ſink, themſelves, into obſcure
graves, unwept, and unremembered,
without a tongue to ſpeak their
worth, or a ſtone to record their virtues.

In

In time of peace, thofe evils are ftill more fevere; for in war, not only the fword cuts itfelf a paffage to preferment, but thofe high born, and rich competitors leave the field when it is ftained with blood. But how many regiments are continually languifhing in our baneful colonies? How many officers of courage, and experience, are finking under the rage of unremitting fkies, without the rewards of their fervice, mean and inadequate as they are?

No fooner does the news of a death, by the fword, or by the elements, arrive in England, than the levee rooms fhine with cofmetic complections, and unfullied fcarlet; the votes of their kindred are weighed in the minifterial balance, and the parchment is depofited in the finking fcale. The facred mouths of bleeding wounds, and the memorials of faithful fervice,

are

are but silent and unavailing re-
proaches; they plead in vain, when
there are no hearts to receive their im-
preffions; they are diftant, and are neglected; they are paft, and are forgot-
ten.

It is only upon the ufeful and valuable part of the army that all its grievances fall. To the ftripling of the peaceable parade, it is the limbo of vanity;
to the veteran of the field, it is a path
fown with thorns. The gay young
enfign, with fupport and intereft, is
like a veffel in port, fleeping on the
peaceful bofom of the waters, and
flaunting with her ftreamers; the old
and neglected officer is the difmafted
hulk, driving with the blaft, and fight-
ing with the billows.

After a ten years peace the very
ideas of fervice are obliterated; the
furvivors of the war are moftly re-
tired to obfcure corners, where luxury

has

has not yet fpread her lateft banners, where their pay will ftill fupply the cravings of nature, and cover their nakednefs ; thofe that remain, without money, or intereft, having the mortification to be commanded by boys whom they have feen at the breaft, lofe all their military ardour, and retire at laft, difgufted by conftant difappointment; ferving as beacons to the wife, to fhun entering the lifts for a country, where contempt and forrow are the prizes.

Their places in the army are fupplied by perfons of two denominations: the firft, as I have already obferved, do not often embrace it as a profeffion, but fly to it as a refuge from idlenefs, or oftener as a fanction for it ; inftead of accomplifhing themfelves in the fciences which form the bafis of the military art, they confume their time in the fafhionable debaucheries,

debaucheries, and a few years courfe enervates their minds, and enfeebles their bodies, fo as to render them totally unfit for the duties of their profeffion, which, however lightly confidered from fuch humble reprefentatives, demands the exertion of the rareft and moft confummate abilities, feldom liberally beftowed by nature, and ftill feldomer perfected by ftudy.

The fecond denomination of officers are fuch as have little or no dependence but on the army, who have received, or purchafed their firft commiffion, and who, as the younger fons of noblemen, (do not chufe to kifs the b—ch of a minifter,) of gentlemen, or of perfons in trade, have perhaps two thoufand pounds for their patrimony, which, in procefs of time, is funk for the purchafe of a company ; *and there the profpect fhuts.* For without both money and intereft,

F   (and

(and often the firſt, though ſupported by long ſervice, will not do,) there is now rarely any inſtance of further preferment. So that thoſe men who ſeriouſly attach themſelves to the military profeſſion, have ſeldom an opportunity of diſtinguiſhing themſelves, or of ſerving effectually their country ; they are almoſt univerſally commanded by men of the firſt mentioned claſs, who are not in general ſoldiers in ſpirit, principle, or capacity. Military preferments, like other important truſts, are now merely diſpoſed of as annuities, by that Gorgon of corruption, ſtiled parliamentary intereſt, and come into the long liſt of jobs, which ſwallow up every thing that is decent, or honourable.

The guards deſerve a place here, as finiſhing the climax of oppreſſion and abuſe. I do not mean to draw
any

any low invidious parallels betwen the foldiers of the court, and the camp, or to examine into their comparative deferts. There are many officers in the guards, who would do honour to any military corps: but I muſt attack the inſtitution as injurious, and unjuſt. The fuperior rank which the guards have over the line, cannot be defended on any principle of military policy.

To give an additional luſtre to the appendages of royalty, is not only proper, but neceſſary; men in all degrees, being equal in capacity and frailty, the dignity of power and government muſt be gloſſed over with every varniſh which ferves to dazzle the optics of the multitude: a king fhould never throw off the purple, or unbind the jewels from his brow. The painted roof, the gilded equipage, the grove of white and yellow fticks,

the

the rainbow of ribbands, and the firmament of stars, have all their origin in use. The dignity of royal attendance is authorized by the custom of all nations. Let the lieutenants of the guards then be captains, and let the captains be colonels, nay generals, or field marshals if they please; but let them be a distinct body from the line of the marching army; and as their duties are entirely different, let their rewards not clash with each other: let not the safe silken service of a court, however honourable, supersede the hazardous and laborious duties of the camp.

The rise in the guards is so rapid, from the suppression of the ranks of lieutenant, and major, that the officers of the line have always the mortification to find, after long and painful service, a body of men, nursed in the bosom of peace, who supersede them

in

in their profeffion, and claim, from abfolute military rank, and feniority, moft of the elevated pofts in the army. And while they are braving all the hoftile elements, where our commerce calls for protection; while they are fuffering the difappointments and re-tardments already ennumerated, from the fuperior interefts of many mem-bers of their own body; when time and patience have at laft removed thefe obftacles, and the road feems fmooth towards a regiment, an innundation of captains in the guards, who,(whatever may be their genius or merit, have had no opportunities of acquiring mi-litary fkill, and who can have no rea-fonable claim to promotion in the line,) by dint of court rank, and eti-quette of precedency, ftep in between, defeat all the profpects of the actual foldier, and trample upon a life of

dangers,

dangers, fatigues, and important fervice to the public.

Befides all the hardfhips and injuftices already touched upon, there feems to be a total want of art and policy in the government of the army. Honour being the very aliment of a foldier, all wife nations have annexed particular rewards to military merit, and fervice; which though not intrinfic, and confequently not burthenfome to the ftate, have yet roufed and fupported a greater heroic fpirit among troops, than the richeft treafury could effect. There is no fhadow of this fenfible policy in Great Britain; and the caufe generally affigned for this neglect is, that we are a commercial nation, a free people, and that thefe baits for military emulation can only be made refpectable in defpotic and monarchical governments, by the fole will of the prince. But this objection

tion is almost too abfurd to demand a refutation. Merit, real, or fuppofed, of all kinds, is rewarded in England, by the orders of knighthood; and thofe diftinctions, though not intrinfic, and though rendered in fome meafure contemptible from the moft unworthy proftitutions, are yet objects of greater and more univerfal ambition, than higher dignities, and more fubftantial gratifications. Why are there then no public teftimonies of merit for the foldier? The order of the Bath it is true was inftituted for this purpofe, (as in fact all orders originally were,) and its fword fhould never be girt but on the warrior; but this rule is not adhered to. His majefty has indeed lately invefted feveral moft refpectable companions; Sir Eyre Coote, Sir John Lindfay, Sir Robert Keith, Sir Adolphus Oughton, reflect great honour on the order:

Sir

Sir Edward Hawke, Sir Jeffrey Amherst, Sir Charles Saunders, and Sir George Pococke, are a group that render it sacred. But the distinction is leſſened by misapplication; is sullied, and tarniſhed by corruption. The petty envoys at the secondary courts, (who are little better than gentlemen uſhers to Engliſh fools, who ſquander their fortunes in foreign countries,) like the jay in the fable, are adorned with this wreath of the ſoldier; Lord ********** carries it about with him to the ſtews; and a Weſt India ſugar-planter glitters among his hogſheads and his negroes with a ſtar which ſhould only beam upon the hero's breaſt.

But were even all the ſtalls of this military order properly filled, ſomething more is wanting; ſome nearer and more general object of emulation; ſomething which tells the public that the

I

the wearer has devoted himself so long to the service of his country, and that merit has distinguished his service. Nothing is so dear to a worthy breast as honest fame: an iron badge of glory is a greater prize to a soldier than an ingot of gold ; it is an absolute talisman, which inspires heroism, and creates honour ; and, so long as it remains uncorrupted, it is, in my mind, though on the breast of a private centinel, a nobler, a more respectable, a more enviable trophy, than the irradiated star on a titled and a pensioned slave.

It was sentiments like these that raised the Romans to universal empire, and could they happily have preserved them, and resisted the allurements of luxury, the Goths might still have inhabited the deserts of the North, and Rome might have yet been the mistress of the world. But in governments where corruption has

G   made

made any great ftrides, there can be no rewards devifed, or inftituted, for military, or any other fpecies of merit ; becaufe the very fources of honour are contaminated : what luftre can it reflect on a man of worth, and character, to arrive at a diftinction, which money, or anceftry can obtain for a coward, or a flave ?

A military order, like the Croix de St. Louis, which only marks out the years, and not the reputation of fervice, is (though very inferior in its ufes to an order of merit,) unhappily the only fpecies of military dignity which could take place with any fuccefs in Great Britain. The latter would only fwell the already boundlefs current of corruption, " Omnia venalia, omnia exeunt in lucrum." A critical vote to turn the fcale in the fenate would inftal a hero ; a marriage with a lord's whore, or a perjury at a contefted election, would foon overtop the ftorm of a breach, or the taking of a battery.

The high improvement, and good footing of the army, is neverthelefs too univerfally the language of unthinking officers; the changes in the cloathing, the new cock of a hat, a better fancy for the cut of a lapel, or the numeration of a button, have charms for many minds fufficient to efface the dreadful neglect of men who have bled, and whofe fathers have died for their country; and to caft a fhade over abufes, neglects, and oppreffions of the foldier, which make the army daily degenerate into a wretched banditti, efcaped from goals, and returned from tranfportation, without the enthufiafm of their profeffion, the fpirit to brave its dangers, or the ftrength to fupport its fatigues. I will venture to pronounce, that on its prefent footing, none but idle worthlefs

fcounscoundrels would present themselves in the event of a war; and little dependence is to be had on men who are constrained to serve against their inclinations, and whose education and manners are incompatible with the service.

The evils then, are I think sufficiently proved, and too grievously felt, particularly that of the pay, which is a leading cause of the rest; the question alone is, how it must be rectified? Here men generally stop, from a lamentable defect in the human character: the words which Solomon puts into the mouth of the slothful, are almost the universal language of mankind, when their necessities prompt them to dubious undertakings. " There is a lion in the way, and I shall be slain in the streets." This puerile despondency is the bane both of societies, and individuals, but more eminently

eminently of the firſt; for that the united buſineſs of every body, is the buſineſs of nobody, is true even to a proverb. Each man ſays within him-ſelf, what can I do alone in this affair? Their ſickly imaginations preſent mag-nified and multiplied difficulties; and thus they content themſelves with grumbling and groaning under bur-thens, without trying to ſhake them off.

It ſhould always be remembered, that few permanent and capital ad-vantages have ever accrued to ſociety, from the firſt effort of one individual; that few ample victories have been gained, without many previous de-feats, and new riſings to the charge. In the progreſs of learning, the moſt ſimple and manifeſt truths have, at firſt, only been ſuppoſed poſſible, by ro-mantic imaginations; and in political life, the ſteps to civilization have been ſlow and weariſome, clogged with

painful

painful impediments, and often
overwhelmed in tumultuous deftruc-
tion; yet begun again with vigour,
and executed with patience, have been
crowned with fuccefs. The radiant
path of liberty has been fown with
thorns, and involved in terrors, and
darknefs; by what painful and unremitting toils our illuftrious forefathers have weeded it for their children, without even the reafonable
hope of fuccefs to fweeten their labours, ought to be a theme of rejoicing
and emulation for us.

On thefe principles I reafon, and
on thefe principles I write; I do not
flatter myfelf that my puny labour
will awaken attention, or obtain re-
drefs, yet if it animates but one individual of brighter and more cultivated
talents, and of more general influence, the flame in time may catch,
and the work at laft may be done.

If even that good fortune fhould be wanting, I fhall, at leaft, have the fatisfaction of throwing in my mite to the good of the fociety, of which I think it my greateft honour to be a member: nothing can ravifh from me the more refined pleafure of pleading the caufe of many brave, worthy, neglected men, who have deferved nobly of their country, whofe diftreffes are a ftain on the national character, and whofe private worth and amiable qualities have endeared many of them to myfelf.

The general election* is now juft at hand ; corruption is fometimes a feptennial plant, whofe feeds, fhaken periodically, with the affiftance of golden plough-fhares, prepare the land for a new crop. Every manure which the

* The reader will eafily perceive from the above paragraph, and confequent reafoning, that this pamphlet was written under an idea that the late parliament would not be diffolved till the ufual time ; he will therefore neceffarily make the allowance for the author here fpeaking in the prefent tenfe.

filth of vice can engender, is then laid
to the root of this baleful cultivation.
The people of England, perhaps, are
preparing once more to give a feven
years leafe of their rights and liberties
to the higheft bidders; if fo, I for one,
fhall heartily laugh at their impudent
clamours, when I hear of their future
grievances. He that purchafes at the
price of *money*, has a right to be paid
again *in kind*; and it is a mockery of
common fenfe in the *corrupted*, to expect either virtue or protection at the
hands of their *corruptors*.

But as it is impoffible for a few to
ftem a powerful and confirmed tor-
rent, let us at leaft be wife for ourfelves. Let us not be the only fools
in the community. The army poffefs
a very confiderable intereft in different parts of England, from the fortune, the birth, and connections of
many of its members. Let us huf-
band that intereft for our own advantage.

tage. Alas, every man does fo for his own as an individual, but no one thinks of the community. Public fpirit has breathed its laft among us. Its very name is only to be found in old Greek and Latin books, which very few can now read. If officers will only ufe their influence for their own particular promotions, and neglect every honourable attempt for the good of their body, little can be ex-pected from any combination of the reft. For the misfortune is, that none of the grievances, or abufes com-plained of, affect that part of the ar-my, whofe complaints would have any weight in the fenate of the na-tion : as it is not the force of truth or juftice, but the power and influence of property, that moves the political fprings.

There are, however, among us a refpectable few who are an honour to

H   their

their high rank, and a credit to their profeſſion ; who, in the midſt of affluence, can feel for the diſtreſſes of their fellow-ſoldiers, and the dignity of the army. From theſe men much may be hoped ; their influence in matters of election, and the immediate voice of many of them in the houſe of commons, would put the buſineſs on a ſerious and reſpectable footing, and from the unanimity, firmneſs, and well regulated ſpirit of the reſt, much might be reaſonably expected.

Firſt then, let every officer in the whole body of the army, who has vote, or influence, in the ſenatorial election of Great Britain, refuſe that vote, or intereſt, to any perſon, however nearly connected by blood, alliance, dependence, or expectation, unleſs he binds himſelf on the moſt ſolemn obligations of a man of honour, to forward by his vote and

and by arguments, if a fpeaker, fuch petition of the army for an augmentation of the pay, as may be prefented to the houfe, while he is a member of it. Or if their votes and influence are already engaged, let them demand from the reprefentative, as a point of honour, and the right of a conftituent, what it is too late to infift upon as a ftipulation.

Secondly, let officers of all ranks, not only in Great Britain and Ireland, but in the colonies and foreign garrifons, fubfcribe their names to the following memorial, or any other that may be adopted on maturer confideration. This is what every officer owes to the military community, and what not one can refufe, without expofing himfelf to the contempt and refentment of his corps; for I may venture to affirm, that, in moft regiments

in

in the service, a very great majority would subscribe to any honourable plan for a moderate and equitable augmentation. Let the subscriptions then, when completed, be sent to the agents of the respective regiments, and let a committee be appointed for collecting them together, in order to be presented to the legislature.

Thirdly. Previous to the presenting this memorial to parliament, the throne should be propitiated; for although, in the spirit of the constitution, we are the servants of the nation, yet it is a necessary military tenet to consider ourselves as the more immediate servants of the crown: we receive our commissions from royal authority, and bind ourselves by accepting them, to obedience, which the laws do not prescribe to other subjects. Besides, we have just reason to build great

great expectations on the king's humanity, and juftice, and the great affection he has ever difplayed for his army. The annexed memorial then, fhould be figned in the fame manner as the other, and be prefented to his majefty, by fome officer of diftinction, in the name of the whole; and let the event be dutifully and patiently expected.

A tranfaction of fo ferious and urgent a complection, could never be neglected by the king, or flurred over by parliament. The affair would come formally and ferioufly before the houfe, and we fhould at leaft hear what arguments they could bring to fuftain the propriety of the fhameful abufes complained of; and why one of the moft honourable, and moft ufeful parts of the community fhould be cut off from all the advantages which Britifh fubjects derive from the riches

riches and profperity of the nation. They would tell us at leaft, from what political principle it is neceffary, that the people fhould labour under grievous taxes, for the amaffing of aftonifhing fums, to be employed as the wages of infamy and corruption; for the luxuries of men who are dead weights about the neck of their country, receiving great annuities under the fanction of holding offices which are multiplied fcandaloufly and needlefsly, to ferve the purpofes of corrupt and felfifh miftifters *; they will prove to us at leaft the equity and neceffity of thefe eftablifhments; they will no doubt give us ample reafons why the civil lift is fo immenfely out of proportion to the military funds; and why every clerk in a paltry public of-

---

* I fpeak of the routine of the times, and do not apply to any individuals.

ficc

fice should be enabled to keep his
fille, and drink claret at the nation's
expence; while the officers of the army
can hardly subsist, and the soldiers are
actually starving.

We might further on our parts,
with submission, desire to ask for infor-
mation and instruction, whether it is
necessary that every chancellor, secre-
tary, or other great officer of state
should retire on pensions of three and
four thousand pounds per annum,
with reversions to the third and fourth
generations; and that all persons in
the civil departments of government
should be gratified with ten times
the sum adequate to the importance
of the trusts? and whether such sums
combined together, with many other
deductions from the hoards of corruption, would not be sufficient to re-
dress the grievances of the army,
without further burthen on the nation?

tion? Whether an able financier, with
the rare talents of honefty, and public fpirit, might not make fuch equitable divifion of what the people pay
to government, fo as that the eftablifhment of the army might bear fome
decent proportion to the change of
times, and to civil appointments of the
fame importance to the public.

However thefe points might be'
gloffed over with parliamentary rhe-
toric, or their impoffibilities expofed
from the hackneyed routine of fubfi-
diary calculation; however they might
be beheld as prefumptive queftions to
be propofed to the fupreme body of
the legiflature, yet if their truth fhone
abroad on the unprejudiced part of the
nation, if the voice of reafon and of
juftice anfwered them in our favour,
if unanimity reigned among us, if
we were not deficient in that fpirit
which ought to be the firft gem in

7   the

the compofition of foldiers, I will be bold to fay, that without any mutinous or unconftitutional proceedings, which I hope no perfon will fuppofe me either to counfel, or infinuate, our folicitations would fhortly be crowned with fuccefs.

But to effect this, the fyftem propofed muft be unanimoufly adopted. Petitions to a fecretary at war, or even to a commander in chief, are not only beneath our dignity, on fuch important occafions, but, on the prefent political fyftem, would be like praying to images, and wooden gods, who cannot help us.

One individual, who, whatever his oftenfible office may be, is fometimes ftyled the minifter, who, like Aaron's rod, fwallows up all other rods ; and the numerous departments of ftate, whofe various bufineffes and interefts it is impoffible he fhould adequately know, be-

I   come

come the subordinate engines of his ambition, and are all made subservient to
one great plan of self-preservation in
office. His scheme being thus, to
maintain, rather than to fulfill his sta-
tion, the power and property, not the
capacities and merits of men, must
consequently be the objects of his
scrutiny and favour; and when a ri-
vality becomes critical, and the rotten
fabric begins to totter, no decorum,
regularity, or consistency is any longer
preserved: orders are issued to the
heads of the different departments for
the most preposterous promotions;
they must be indiscriminately obeyed,
or the secondary ministers instantly
make way for creatures of the first; it
is in vain for the oppressed to remon-
strate with the nominal rulers of the
several lines; a peremptory and deci-
sive blow is prepared for remonstrance
and complaint; they are told (and

8   what

what other anfwer can the moft up-
right man give who is not independent) that it is the king's pleafure ;
although he is rarely, and never ho-
neftly confulted on many difgraceful
occafions. His majefty has ever ma-
nifefted the greateft juftice, and the
moft amiable humanity, when the cry
of oppreffed merit has happened to
reach the throne ; but alas! its avenues
are fo blocked up by the dragons and
harpies of ftate, that her low and mo-
deft voice is feldom heard.

It is much to be lamented, that
this abfurd and ruinous ftruggle for
adminiftration fhould thus trample
upon the fundamental principles of
reafon and policy. So long as it ex-
ifts, it is impoffible that vigour and
good order fhould be found in any,
but more efpecially in the military
deparment ; where, if merit and capacity are obliged to ftoop to the un-

I 2 manly

manly intrigue and venality of a
court, *an army is like a lion without teeth
or claws.* No reformation can be rea-
fonably hoped for, till the minifters
for war are made independent of
the civil ftatefman, at leaft in the
eftablifhment, formation, and difpofi-
tion of troops, and the univerfal and
uncontrouled difpofal of military
trufts; no good can be expected, till
a commander in chief is chofen by
the fovereign, on the fole confideration of his military and moral character, never to be dictated to, or removed by a minifter; (and a prince
of the blood, of good difpofitions, is
much to be preferred, in a government like ours, to the moft favourite
fubject.) Thus fet aloof from all political connections and temptations, he
could have no guide but the balance
of juftice, and could never degenerate
into a broker of commiffions, or be
betrayed

betrayed into public breaches of faith
and decency, such as I have formerly beheld, rather with pity than resentment,
when elections and party-rage have
triumphed over the moft feeling
heart, and the moft honeft and amiable difpofitions.

Thefe folecifms in government are
however now become fo familiar, that
to the complaints of fuch general
abufes, and the grievances of deferv-
ing individuals, there is one general
anfwer given. "The conftitution, we
are told, does not always admit of
merits being impartially rewarded, by
even the juftice of the fovereign.
That he too is hemmed in by political obligations, to which he muft
often facrifice even his own pleafure,
and his opinion of right. That what
the king, in the goodnefs of his
heart, would beftow on meritorious
fervice, the minifter has already pro-
mifed

mifed in his mafter's name, to carry on his own felfifh politics, which is dignified with the name of the k——'s bufinefs; and every honeft man who refufes to fall down before the golden calf, is fet forth in odious colours, and is reprefented to his f———n as a dangerous and alienated fubjcct.". Thefe are indeed truths, melancholy and difgraceful truths, but they cannot be charged on the conflitution. The fyftem of Britifh government is the moft fublime fabric of human wifdom and virtue which the annals of the world can produce; the deviation from its fpirit and purity is the moft aweful monument of the folly and infamy of men.

A k——g of G——t B———n, in the true fpirit of the conflitution, may, through the medium of the laws, encourage virtue, and diftribute impartial juftice, more efpecially among that

portion

portion of his fubjects over whom the
royal prerogative has given him the
fole and arbitrary command. Contented with that portion of power
with which the laws inveft him, he
need never entangle himfelf in laby-
rinths of policy, and contentions of
interefts, which pervert the adminiftration of juftice, and fully the facred
luftre of the c—n. His beft charter
being written in the hearts of his
faithful people, the cabals of a minifter would be unneceffary to carry on
the bufinefs of the nation, equally in-
terefting and important to the whole.
The cry of Jealoufy and Faction,
which, from the nature of man, can
never be perfectly hufhed, would be
drowned in the louder voice of Reafon
and Concord; Merit would walk bold-
ly to the throne to receive her wreath,
and Vice, afhamed to fhew her fpotted
face, would hide herfelf in obfcurity.

It

It is under such a government that the army would indeed be a respectable body, an honourable and an eligible profession.

There is nothing in the character of our most excellent k——g repugnant to the fulfillment of this political portrait; on the contrary, I believe it to be the epitome of his wishes; but to carry it into perfect execution, much must be done, and much more be undone; much must be changed, which none but God can change, and which, in the order of his Providence, and his disposition of human affairs, (if we may be allowed to reason from analogy) will almost certainly not happen.

The nation is ripening fast for the inexorable sickle of Time, which moves progressively over the face of the earth, gathers the nations, and casts them into obscurity, for future, and

perhaps

perhaps brighter renovations. Liberty already fits on the weſtern cliffs of Albion, pruning her wing for the vaſt flight of the Atlantic, beyond whoſe foam her infant ſons are ſtretching forth their eager arms to embrace her. From thence ſhe may move on like the ſun in his courſe, illuminate ſtill unknown nations, and return again to thoſe in the ſhadow of darkneſs. Theſe changes however will not probably happen in our times ; and ſoldiers having fewer and leſs fixed poſterity than others, need not extend their proſpects ſo far: " Sufficient for the day is the evil thereof." Enough for us to be wiſe for ourſelves, to live in honour, and in plenty, and to die with glory.

K   F O R M

FORM of a PETITION

H——E of C———N S.

To the Honourable the C—ns of
G—t B—n in P———t affembled:
The humble Petition of the Officers
of the Army whofe Names are
hereunto fubfcribed.

WHEN we reflect on the great
debt in which the nation is
involved, from the neceffary expences
of the late glorious war, the vaft fums
annually levied on the people for the
purpofes of government, and the
heavy taxes which are, in confequence,
laid on every article of univerfal con-

K 2   fumption,

fumption, it is with the ftrongeft re-
luctance that we offer any claim tend-
ing the moft diftantly to encreafe or
aggravate thefe evils. We have fo
deeply at heart the welfare and profperity of our country, that great as
our hardfhips are, they would be entirely abforbed, and fuffered as a
willing facrifice to the general happinefs: and it is only in the hope and
belief that their removal may not be
incompatible with the public good,
that we humbly fubmit our fituation
to your ferious confideration.

The great riches, which, from the
extenfion of commerce and conqueft
have flowed in upon Great Britain
from fo many fources, the confequen-
tial decreafe of the value of money,
the progrefs of luxury, with many
other co-operating caufes, have fo entirely changed the fyftem of things
fince the firft eftablifhment of the pay ;
the

the prices of all the abfolute neceffaries of life have augmented in fo
prodigious a ratio; fo many new
wants have arifen, by cuftom confirmed into neceffities, that what was
originally granted by the nation, as a
proper independence to fupport the
dignity of the army, is now abfolute-
ly incompatible with the fulfilment
of fuch intention, in all the military
degrees under a regiment; and is in
the fubaltern ranks altogether inadequate to the fingle article of fub-
fiftence, independent of the many expences unavoidably incurred, in com-
pliance with the regulations of military parade, without which an army
cannot exift.

The truth of thefe circumftances is
of fuch public notoriety, that we
think it unneceffary to enlarge upon
them, more efpecially before this au-
guft affembly, where every individual

dual muft be perfectly acquainted with points which fo nearly concern the public welfare.

We cannot help feeing with chagrin, and mortification, that the falaries of all the fervants of the nation in civil trufts, the emoluments of every fpecies of public bufinefs, have, in fome meafure, kept pace with the changes of the times, (the army alone excepted;) and that in confequence of fuch diftribution, there is no equable proportion obferved between civil and military trufts, of equivalent importance to the ftate ; vaft fums being annually appropriated to the fupport of the holders of the former in all the luxuries of life, while the latter are fuffering all the rigours of neceffity and poverty.

As we confider ourfelves as a very refpectable branch of the people, whofe ftewards you are, we think ourfelves

fully

fully juftified, in offering, with fub-
miffion, thefe points to your ferious
and immediate attention, and in praying for relief with refpect to our pay,
which the rapid progreffion of the
circumftances, already enumerated,
renders every day more urgent, and
which cannot be much longer neglected, without the difaffection and
total ruin of the army.

We pray that our legal and duti-
ful petition may not be confidered as
the remonftrance of a mercenary
body, who, knowing their own ufe
and importance, would raife their
prices according to the complexion
of the times; we are honourable vo-
lunteers in the fervice of a free
country, to which we would as chear-
fully facrifice our fortunes as our
lives; but as the moft numerous,
and moft important part of us, the

7   real

real foldiers of the army, have no re-
fources in private property, we are
obliged to afk fuch fupport from the
nation, to whofe defence and independence we dedicate ourfelves, as may
enable us to perform the duties we
owe her, with a dignity fuitable to the
rank in which we are placed by our
king, and the relation in which we
ftand to the ftate.

But in what manner, and in what
proportion thefe our humble wifhes
may be beft effected, we fubmit entirely to the wifdom, the humanity,
and the juftice of parliament.

It is the abfolute fting of neceffity,
and not any mutinous, or illegal fpirit, which dictates this plain and
pointed memorial. We are deeply
impreffed with the fenfe of the facred
ties which link men together under
the authority of laws, and we pray
that

that the unfettered language of
truth, may not be miftaken for the
gauntlet of defiance, which we never
can throw down but to the enemies
of our country.

Signed

L   FORM

FORM of a PETITION

TO THE

K —— —— G,

To the K——G's Moft Excellent M——
——Y : The humble Petition of the
Officers of the Army whofe Names
are hereunto fubfcribed.

S I R E,

WHEN any civil order of the
community is opprefled, or
neglected, they muft (though under
the protection of the fovereign,) have
recourfe to the laws. If the laws are
defective, they cannot hope for re-
drefs, but in the procraftination of
amendments or new inftitutions ; and

the

the private fubject in the beft regulated governments muft often fuffer
by the delays infeparable from the
execution of civil juftice:

It is the peculiar privilege of military bodies, to look immediately up
to the fource of power, and it is the
particular happinefs of the Britifh
army that this fource, in the facred
perfon of your Majefty, is likewife
the unfullied fource of juftice. In-
fomuch that we cannot even reflect
with regret on the immunities of
freedom which the civil fubjects of
Great Britain fo amply poffefs, and
which we as foldiers in many points
forego, when we confider that of
the code to which our lives and our
honours are fubjected, your Majefty
is the fole and ultimate judge, in
whofe royal breaft we can repofe
our neareft concerns, as in the bofom of a father.

The

The great changes which thefe
kingdoms, and indeed all Europe, have
undergone fince your Majefty's royal
anceftors fixed the eftablifhment of
the army of Great Britain, have ex-
tended themfelves equably and pro-
portionally ; the value of lands, the
rates of labour, the profits of manufactures, the prices of commodities,
and the falaries of perfons in civil
trufts, public or private, have all kept
pace with the decreafe of the value of
money, occafioned by commerce and
conqueft. The luxuries of the age
have been a fpur to induftry and in-
vention ; have rewarded and encou-
raged the arts, and have been an
ample fource of riches and improvement. The fyftem of life has been
gradually and uniformly elevated to
a greater fcale, from the natural progrefs of fociety, and has left the
army fingly behind it in its priftine
con-

condition, as a folitary, and melancholy ftandard of thofe changes.
Subjecting it to defray (with the
humble funds allotted in an age
when the treafuries of monarchs did
not always amount to the riches of
many of your Majefty's private fubjects,) all the expences which the ha-
bits of luxury have confirmed into
neceffities, when even the moft fimple
and indifpenfable demands of life,
are not from the above mentioned
changes within the compafs of its
eftablifhment.

The great expences in which the
late glorious war involved Great Britain, has long with-held us from in-
truding thefe our diftreffes on the
attention of your Majefty, and the
nation. A thirteen years ftate of
tranquillity and commerce now em-
boldens us to declare them at the
foot

foot of the throne, and before the affembly of the people.

We are fo well affured of your Majefty's good difpofitions towards your faithful and affectionate army, that we would willingly rely fingly on them upon this occafion ; but as the forms of the conftitution inveft the people's reprefentatives with the fole right of levying the neceffary fupplies for the fupport of government, we have framed a memorial to be delivered to them, affembled in parliament, demanding, as a collective body, that equitable dividend of the public funds, which our ufe and importance to the nation entitle us to expect. In order by thefe means to fhew, that it is not your Majefty who would burthen your fubjects in general, for an additional fupport of your more immediate fervants ; but that we, as

the

the defenders of the ſtate, as well as the protectors of the throne; as the guardians of the people, as well as the miniſters of the crown; as a part of the community, laboriouſly devoted to the ſafety and independence of the whole—do of ourſelves call upon the nation for that ſupport which her riches, procured by the ſucceſs of our arms, in the protection of her commerce, enable her to afford; and which the changes ſuch riches have produced, have rendered indiſpenſably neceſſary for the exiſtence of the army.

As a body ourſelves of the people, we have thus adjudged it to be our right to ſpeak our minds freely, but reſpectfully, to their repreſentatives; to your Majeſty we addreſs ourſelves with the humility of ſervants, and with the affection of children. Sentiments which ariſe not only from

the

the duty we owe to the King whom it has pleafed the Almighty to appoint to rule over us ; but from thofe princely virtues, and that benevolence of character, which temper the aufterity of power with the mildnefs of humanity ; and which unite in our hearts a love for the man, with a veneration for the fovereign.

Signed

F I N I S.